# Liv & Di

# Liv & Di

## A Play

## John Dufresne

New York, New York

Copyright © 2019 John Dufresne

All rights reserved. No part of this book may be reproduced, scanned, or distributed in any printed or electronic format without permission.

Published by MidTown Publishing Inc.
1001 Avenue of Americas
12th Floor
New York, NY 10018

Library of Congress Control Number: 2019941927

**ISBN 978-1-62677-021-8** (print book)

All rights reserved
Printed in the United States of America
First Edition
1 3 5 7 9 10 8 6 4 2

To Cindy, who makes it all possible

# Liv & Di

By

**John Dufresne**

# Liv & Di

*Liv & Di* was produced at the WCLOC THEATER COMPANY, Worcester, Massachusetts, June 13-16, 2019. The play was produced by Jo Ann Savage and directed by Linda Oroszko.

## The Original Cast

| | |
|---|---|
| DIANE | Kate Moylan |
| LIVINGSTON | Kevin Moylan |
| VITA | Caitlin Lahey |
| FINN | John Morello |
| ANNA/CADDY | Monica Borci |
| 45 | Nick Leonelli |
| MAN/RUDY | Vic Kruczynski |
| MIMI | Lisa Mielnicki |

# CHARACTERS

DIANE MOODY Her marriage is trending to disorder.

LIVINGSTON MOODY Diane's husband thinks he has a remedy for the marriage blues.

VITA has her own problems with a philandering husband.

FINN Vita's philandering husband.

ANNA a dichotomist with principles.

45 a golfer with a hefty handicap.

CADDY, 45's gal Friday.

MAN emotionally attached to his smartphone.

RUDY 45's chauffeur.

MIMI the Moodys' personal assistant device

## SCENE

Worcester, Massachusetts

## TIME
During the Reign of 45

## ACT I

*(DIANE and LIVINGSTON MOODY's bedroom. At center stage, a bed, the back raised to a sitting-up position. At stage right a door to the bathroom. At stage left a door to the rest of the house. Downstage right a vanity with three mirrors and a seat. Downstage left a cafe table and two chairs. On the table are a bottle of wine and two wine glasses. Upstage right a hat and coat rack. In front of the bed, a storage chest with cushion. Two night tables beside the bed. On Diane's table (stage right) are her cell phone, a lamp, a stack of magazines, and a book. On Livingston's table, an iPad, an unobtrusive personal assistant device, and a lamp.)*

*(Diane's phone lights up and plays "By the Sea." LIVINGSTON enters carrying a book. He looks at the phone, checks the caller, does not answer.)*

LIVINGSTON:
    *(Falsetto)*
Hi, you've reached the Moodys. This is Diane ...
    *(Baritone)*
And this is Livingston butting in ...
    *(Falsetto)*
I can't come to the phone right now, but leave a message and I'll call you back.

*(LIVINGSTON sits on the storage chest and reads.)*

DIANE: Liv, honey, who was on the phone?

LIVINGSTON: Vita.

*(DIANE enters in a long night dress. She sits at the vanity and brushes her hair.)*

DIANE: She and Finn are going through a rough patch.
    *(Pause)*
Vita found out about Finn's indiscretion with what's-her-face. You know, the phlebotomist.

*(LIVINGSTON holds up his book.)*

LIVINGSTON: Einstein.

DIANE No, I think it's Pollock. Something Something Pollock. Like the fish. Pollachius pollachius.

*(He gives her a quizzical look.)*

LIVINGSTON: When Einstein was dying, when he was taking his last breath, he barely managed to say something to the nurse in the room. The last words of the smartest man in the world. His final thought. How wonderful there was someone there to hear him. Only he spoke in German, and the American nurse didn't understand him.

DIANE: Ann Marie. Ann Marie Pollack. Or Mary Ann. Mary Pat Trout?

LIVINGSTON: I wonder what my last words will be?

*(DIANE examines herself in the mirror, points to herself and to her reflected selves in turn.)*

DIANE: There are four of me.

*(LIVINGSTON dips his finger into an imaginary jar and licks the finger. He holds his stomach and gags.)*

LIVINGSTON: How long has this mayonnaise been out?

*(DIANE adjusts a side mirror.)*

DIANE: Two mirrors make a labyrinth. The vanity and I go on forever.

*(LIVINGSTON reaches down as if to pick something off the floor.)*

LIVINGSTON:
>(Falsetto)
Don't worry, dear, it's just a telephone cable.

(*LIVINGSTON grabs the imagined wire, is shocked into convulsion and feigns death.*)

DIANE: Forever.
>(Pause)
What a dreadful thought.

(*LIVINGSTON snaps his fingers.*)

LIVINGSTON: That's how long infinity lasts.
>(Pause)
If the universe is infinite then everything that could happen must happen. There is a married couple who are us on a blue planet in a distant galaxy, only he's the nurse, and she's the physicist.

DIANE: You're a therapist.
>(Pause)
Not a physicist. That was your dream. You couldn't do the math.

LIVINGSTON: Word problems.

DIANE: If every day you walk six miles in one hour and fifty minutes, and your friend Chris walks eight miles at the same pace, how long will it take Chris to walk his eight miles?

LIVINGSTON: Why doesn't Chris want to walk with me?

DIANE: So you're saying there's a world like this one where I am childless and fit and another world where I get cancer and have children but don't live to see them grow up?

LIVINGSTON: But only if the universe is infinite.

DIANE: And if it's not?

LIVINGSTON: You can choose where you want to be, but not when you want to be.

DIANE: That doesn't make sense.

LIVINGSTON: That's the quantum world for you.

DIANE: I can choose when. I can remember my childhood and go there. I can imagine myself in Paris next spring and go there.
 *(Eyes closed)*
It's a bright sunny day, and we're eating chocolate crepes and strolling along the Seine.

LIVINGSTON: No, dear, you can move through space, but not through time.

DIANE: Well, Einstein, I moved through twenty-four hours of time since yesterday.
 *(Pause)*
You live in a theoretical universe.

LIVINGSTON: Some of the time.

DIANE: And I live in the real universe.

LIVINGSTON: But what is real?

*(DIANE gazes into the mirror.)*

DIANE: I can see you.

LIVINGSTON: Not the real me. You see the virtual me, your husband laterally inverted and untouchable.

*(LIVINGSTON picks up the book on Diane's table.)*

LIVINGSTON: The Biology of Marine Life.

DIANE: I'm going to set up a salt-water aquarium.

LIVINGSTON: Who's going to take care of it?

DIANE: They take care of themselves.

LIVINGSTON: Like the body builders at the gym?

DIANE: I'm worried about Vita and Finn.

LIVINGSTON: I'll tell you what's annoying. The way they talk to each other through the dog.
    *(Pause)*
What's the dog's name?

DIANE: Why do people blame nurses for everything. Einstein should have spoken English if he was so smart.

LIVINGSTON: Bullet.
    *(Falsetto.)*
Bullet, tell your daddy that Mommy wants to go to the movies tonight.
    *(Baritone.)*
Bullet, you tell your mommy there's a Sox game on TV tonight.

*(Phone plays "By the Sea." DIANE answers. LIVINGSTON puts down the book, exits to the bathroom.)*

DIANE: Hello.
    *(Listens.)*
Well, you just have to calm down now, hon.

LIVINGSTON: (O.S.) We're out of mouthwash, Di. Where's the mouthwash?

DIANE: Finn's just going through a mid-life thingy, that's all. It happens to all of them. Hold on.
    *(to Livingston)*

Liv, don't leave a mess in there. I just cleaned.
    *(to Vita)*
It won't do any good holding it in. You need to get it off your chest.
    *(Pause)*
Well, that just doesn't add up.

*(LIVINGSTON enters, reading on his iPad.)*

LIVINGSTON: She said, nonplussed.
    *(off Diane's look)*
She figured?

DIANE: You call me when he comes home. Promise.

LIVINGSTON: So this guy in Old Furnace shot himself in the head twice with a flare gun.

DIANE: How did he miss the first time?

LIVINGSTON: You can't do a decent job without the right tools.

DIANE: Did he die?

LIVINGSTON: In the fire--he burned the house down.
    *(Reading)*
Leaves a wife of twenty years and a son at the special school in New Braintree.

DIANE: What would drive a person to do such a thing?

LIVINGSTON: Desperation.

DIANE: I mean what was the precipitating event? The straw that broke the camel's back. The last drop that made the cup run over.

LIVINGSTON: I'll go out on a limb and guess that their marriage had run off the rails.

(*During the following exchange LIVINGSTON takes off his shirt and pants and hangs them on the rack. He's down to his T-shirt, shorts, socks, and slippers. DIANE applies lotions and creams to her face and arms.*)

LIVINGSTON: I remember our first night in this house.

DIANE: Mattress on the floor.

LIVINGSTON: We were so in love, we didn't care.

DIANE: No heat, middle of February!

LIVINGSTON: We stayed nice and toasty.

DIANE: That was such an extraordinary moment, such an overwhelming feeling of surrender, like being swept away on a wave of euphoria.
 (*Pause*)
I felt like you and I were ... coherent, harmonious, bound together.
 (*Pause*)
I knew from that moment on we would always be together, even when we were apart. If I was here and you were at work or in New Zealand or on Mars and you thought of me and turned to your left, as if to see me, I would turn to my right to return your gaze.
 (*Pause*)
I was never more certain of anything in my life.

LIVINGSTON: But you'd have no way to prove you were right.

DIANE: Why would I need proof? Emotions can't lie.
 (*Pause*)
Did you feel the same way?

LIVINGSTON: That was a long time ago.

DIANE: I don't feel like that anymore.

LIVINGSTON: We've de-cohered.

DIANE: If we are apart, we are lost to each other.
    *(Pause)*
I can know where you are but not where you're going.

LIVINGSTON: I'm always coming back to you.

DIANE: Or where you're headed but not where you are.

LIVINGSTON: That night we decided we were going to have three kids, remember?

DIANE: Poppy.

LIVINGSTON: Malayne.

DIANE: Justine.
    *(Pause)*
Why didn't we have them?

LIVINGSTON: Let's not go there again.

DIANE: We could have had one at least. Poppy.

LIVINGSTON: It wasn't in the cards.

DIANE: I miss them.

LIVINGSTON: You can't miss what you never had.

DIANE: I can. I do.
    *(Pause)*
Terribly.

(*DIANE walks to the cafe table and sits. She holds up a bottle. During the following exchange LIVINGSTON and DIANE repel each other like the south poles of two magnets. When she approaches, he retreats. And vice-versa. When she makes eye contact, he looks away, and so on.*)

DIANE: Cabernet?

LIVINGSTON: She whined.

(*She pours two glasses and LIVINGSTON approaches and sits. She stands and steps away. They toast.*)

LIVINGSTON: To us and nobody else.

DIANE: I talk to them.

LIVINGSTON: Who?

DIANE: The kids.

LIVINGSTON: You're starting to freak me out.

DIANE: I don't feel so alone.

LIVINGSTON: I'm here.

DIANE: Are you?

(*DIANE walks to the table. LIVINGSTON stands, crosses behind her.*)

LIVINGSTON: How are they doing?

DIANE: Well, you know, try to get a word out of any of them.

LIVINGSTON: Do they ask about me?

DIANE: I keep them abreast.

(*And with that he gives DIANE a playful leer.*)

LIVINGSTON: We were going to buy a farm in Maine, remember? Be self-sufficient and all that *Mother Earth News* kind of thing.

DIANE: Build stone walls.

LIVINGSTON: Tap for maple syrup. Keep bees. Chop wood. Stalk the wild asparagus.

DIANE: Raise the kids close to nature.

LIVINGSTON: It was all a fancy dream, but that's all it was. Romantic. Impractical.

DIANE: We would have starved. You can't even change a light bulb.

(*DIANE finishes her wine.*)

DIANE: We settled.

LIVINGSTON: We were prudent.

DIANE: Is that any way to run a life?

LIVINGSTON: First we thought we were something on a stick. Then we realized we were not the popular kids.

DIANE: And that took the wind out of our sails, didn't it?

LIVINGSTON: We're mixing our metaphors.

DIANE: So, Liv, I think we should talk about it. About you know what.

LIVINGSTON: About the recent unpleasantness? I thought we

were going to ... you know ... get frisky, fool around some.

(*He lounges on the bed and indicates the ample space beside him.*)

DIANE: Frisky happens before a shower. You know the house rules.

LIVINGSTON: Let's break some rules.

DIANE: Do you know how much these creams cost?

LIVINGSTON: Don't tell me.

DIANE: Plenty. There's a price to pay for looking this gorgeous.

LIVINGSTON: Why would you want to talk about it? You're the felonious one. I'm willing to let it slide. Lesson learned. No need to embarrass you.

DIANE: That's not how marriages are built. They're built on honesty and trust.

LIVINGSTON: That's a lie.

DIANE: Is not.

LIVINGSTON: A falsehood. A misconception. A pipe dream.

DIANE: Talk!

LIVINGSTON: Okay, you start.

DIANE: Let's rewind, shall we.
 (*Pause*)
You pushed me out of the car.

LIVINGSTON: You jumped.

DIANE: We were going fifty.

LIVINGSTON: We were parked. In our driveway.

DIANE: Lucky I wasn't hurt.

LIVINGSTON: You landed on your head.

DIANE: You were trying to kill me.

LIVINGSTON: I saved you from a night in jail.

DIANE: I was innocent.

(*LIVINGSTON opens the drawer of his bedside table and takes out electric scissors.*)

LIVINGSTON: Exhibit A, Your Honor.
    (*Pause*)
When Gary Leblanc tapped you on the shoulder, you had these cordless electric scissors down your pants. Good thing he called me and not the police.

DIANE: I needed the right tool for the job. Beautiful, aren't they? Power trigger, safety switch, lithium-ion technology.

(*She reaches for the scissors, but LIVINGSTON stands and holds them over his head.*)

LIVINGSTON: What job was that?

DIANE: Cutting your hair.

LIVINGSTON: Why?

DIANE: It's your best feature.

LIVINGSTON: That hurts.

(*LIVINGSTON slips the scissors into the drawer and stands guard.*)

LIVINGSTON: Why not pay for them?

DIANE: I had just parked the Bronco outside Ace Hardware when I realized I hadn't brought my purse, my wallet, nothing.

LIVINGSTON: And it wasn't your Bronco. That car belongs to Jimmy Wells. That's a felony right there. Grand theft auto.

DIANE: I knew Jimmy wouldn't press charges. I know too damn much about his "secret" life.

LIVINGSTON: What secret life?

DIANE: Let's just say it's leverage where Mr. Wells is concerned. And I know he keeps a spare key in a magnetic case on the undercarriage of the Bronco.

LIVINGSTON: How do you know that?

DIANE: I pay attention.

LIVINGSTON: So having already stolen a vehicle, you thought it was okay to steal the scissors.

DIANE: Maybe I shouldn't have had that third drink.

LIVINGSTON: What set you off anyway?

DIANE: You did.

LIVINGSTON: I did? How?

DIANE: I was going through your wallet—

LIVINGSTON: Why?

DIANE: I had my reasons.

LIVINGSTON: Looking for leverage?

DIANE: And I found Mary Faford's business card with her cell phone number written on the back.

LIVINGSTON: Mary works in the jewelry department at JCPenney's and said she could get me a deal on a string of pearls for your birthday.

DIANE: Do I look like pearls to you? I'm gold, honey.

LIVINGSTON: And when were you going through my wallet?

DIANE: When you fell asleep on the couch right after supper. After I slaved over the stove all afternoon making you lasagna.
    (*Pause*)
You show your gratitude by burping, farting, and passing out.
    (*Pause*)
That's when I had my first Sunnydriver.
    (*off his look*)
Smirnoff and Sunny D.

LIVINGSTON: I was exhausted. I'd worked a twelve-hour shift at the office. I had two bipolars, an anorexic, a schizophrenic, a depressive, a woman with cyclothymic disorder, my OCD client, and a guy who says God disagrees with my treatment plan for him.
    (*Pause*)
The meal was delicious, by the way. It's my favorite. You haven't made it in a while.

DIANE: I made it as penance for my jealousy.

LIVINGSTON: What do you mean?

DIANE: I saw you at Julie and Angie's wedding.

LIVINGSTON: We were together.

DIANE: I saw your cheating eyes follow Mary's ginormous caboose across the hall.

LIVINGSTON: You imagined it.

DIANE: That's what I thought at the time—I mean who could not look at the junk in that gal's trunk, defying the laws of physics. Until I saw that card in your wallet. That's when I had my second drink.

LIVINGSTON: So my innocent glance—

DIANE: Lecherous.

LIVINGSTON: . . . a week ago began a series of events that led to your attempted robbery of Ace Hardware last night?

DIANE: Exactly. We live life forward, but we understand it backward.

LIVINGSTON: Why do you think I'd be looking at—

DIANE: Lusting after.

LIVINGSTON: . . . other women?

DIANE: Because you're a man.

LIVINGSTON: And all men are alike?

DIANE: Women need to feel loved. Men need to feel flesh.

LIVINGSTON: That's unfair.

DIANE: Can you say "I love you"?

LIVINGSTON: Love you.

DIANE: "I love you."

LIVINGSTON: Love you, too.

DIANE: You can't say it.

LIVINGSTON: I just did.

DIANE: Say "I love you."

LIVINGSTON: Love you.

DIANE: There's a difference.

LIVINGSTON: What?

DIANE: "I."

LIVINGSTON: Me?
    (*Pause*)
Me?
(*The personal assistant device, MIMI, on Livingston's table lights up.*)

DIANE: Not "me." "I."

MIMI: I don't understand the question.

LIVINGSTON: Mimi, stop!

MIMI
    (*Sings*)
In the name of love . . .

DIANE: Mimi, stop!
    (*Pause*)
She listens to me.

(*LIVINGSTON opens his bedside drawer and takes out his sleeping equipment. He reclines on the bed. DIANE picks up a magazine and sits on the bed.*)

LIVINGSTON: Mimi, what's tomorrow's weather forecast?

MIMI: The red wheelbarrow will glaze with rain.

DIANE: We should have spent the extra money for Alexa.

LIVINGSTON: Mimi has a poetic flair.

(*The following bit by LIVINGSTON is performed broadly and played for laughs with exaggerated and embellished hand movements and a fastidiousness beyond what is called for. Through it all, DIANE watches, puzzled and increasingly impatient. Think Ed Norton and Ralph Kramden. He stuffs earplugs into his ears.*)

LIVINGSTON: Hello, hello! Testing 1-2-3.

(*He adjusts the plugs.*)

LIVINGSTON: Barbara Bottner bought some better butter, but she said the better butter's bitter

(*More adjustments.*)

LIVINGSTON: Around the rugged rocks the ragged rascal ran.

(*He clears his throat, coughs up loose phlegm, snorts, grunts, puts a nasal strip on his nose, and breathes freely.*)

LIVINGSTON: Ahh!

(*He fits a mouth guard over his teeth, works his jaw around until he's satisfied. He puts on his eye mask, moves his head around to insure total darkness.*)

DIANE: What the hell are you doing?

(*She shakes his arm.*)

DIANE: Liv!

(*He lifts his mask, says something unintelligible.*)

LIVINGSTON: Wahs so wah?

(*Takes out the mouth guard.*)

LIVINGSTON: What?

DIANE: What is all ... this?

LIVINGSTON: Can't hear you.
    (*off her look*)
Ah, yes.

(*Takes out the plugs.*)

DIANE: You are . . . ?

LIVINGSTON: Going to sleep.

DIANE: On what planet?

LIVINGSTON: You said no fooling around.

DIANE: Can't we talk?

LIVINGSTON: I talk during sex.

DIANE: You give directions.

LIVINGSTON: Just trying to be helpful.

DIANE: How badly do you want sex right now on a scale of 1 or 10?

LIVINGSTON: Eight.

DIANE: Then you'll live.
  (*Pause*)
Did you hear that?

LIVINGSTON: Hear what?

DIANE: That.

LIVINGSTON: No.

DIANE: Someone's outside.

(*They sit up and listen, eyes wide, mouths agape. Nothing.*)

LIVINGSTON: What are you reading?

DIANE: Cosmo. Marriage compatibility test.

LIVINGSTON: Did you ace it?

DIANE: Question #1: My spouse doesn't keep secrets from me. You answer. A. Definitely true. B. Definitely not true. C. Mostly true. D. Mostly not true.

LIVINGSTON: Pass. Let's come back to that question.

DIANE: Are you saying you do keep secrets?

LIVINGSTON: Depends what you mean by "secret."

DIANE: Hidden knowledge.

LIVINGSTON: Truish.

DIANE: What secret?

LIVINGSTON: It's only a secret if you keep it.

DIANE: Secrets are destructive.

LIVINGSTON: They keep the peace.

DIANE: I feel like I don't really know you now.

LIVINGSTON: Secrets can't hurt anyone. But their disclosure can.

DIANE: Tell me your secret.

LIVINGSTON: Aren't I allowed a little privacy?

DIANE: Why would you keep a secret from me?

LIVINGSTON: Shame. Some secrets you take to your grave. You couldn't live with yourself if anyone knew.

DIANE: Question #3. What is your reaction when your spouse enters the room? A. I'm so glad to see you. B. Nothing because you don't notice. C. Why are you here? D. Did you bring me a drink?

LIVINGSTON: A, of course. My turn.

(*He takes the magazine from DIANE.*)

LIVINGSTON: Complete this sentence. My spouse is my blank. A. Best friend. B. Best friend and partner. C. Best friend, partner, and lover. D. Cross to bear.

DIANE: E. All of the above.
    (*Pause*)
Be honest, Liv. Do you think we've fallen into a rut?

LIVINGSTON: Into a routine. Yes.

DIANE: We keep doing the same things over and over. And not doing some things at all. We need to put the spark back into our lives. We need a game changer.

LIVINGSTON: We could get a divorce. That would shake things up.

DIANE: You're not joking?
*(Pause)*
Do you think we could make it work?

LIVINGSTON: Divorce has legs. Half of all marriages end in divorce. How many divorces end in marriage?

DIANE: It would take the pressure off. I could breathe again.

LIVINGSTON: What pressure?

DIANE: Obligations, expectations.
*(Pause)*
Knowing that we don't have to be together but choose to be together will make all the difference.

LIVINGSTON: Divorce is not the end of the world.

DIANE: It will be a new beginning for both of us.

LIVINGSTON: And just because we're divorced doesn't mean we can't live together.

DIANE: Splitting up would just make matters worse.

LIVINGSTON: Dividing up the books, the friends, the furniture, the bank accounts.

DIANE: Unnecessary. Messy.

LIVINGSTON: Ours will be a romantic and benevolent divorce.

DIANE: Lovers, not spouses!

LIVINGSTON: We'll be illicit once again.

DIANE: Living in sin. Is that real enough for you?

LIVINGSTON: Just like when I was courting you, and you were living with your boyfriend what's-his-face, the Realtor.

DIANE: All those afternoons at the Amour Motel in Shrewsbury.

LIVINGSTON: Room 209.

DIANE: I'll call our lawyer in the morning.

LIVINGSTON: The boyfriend did give us a good deal on this house.

(*DIANE takes the magazine from LIVINGSTON and puts it on the floor.*)

DIANE: I don't know if I'll be able to sleep.
    (*Smiles*)
What do you say we get this show on the road.

LIVINGSTON: What do you mean? he asks hopefully.

DIANE: Let's do the deed, get it on, go at it, knock it out, kick it, get lucky, get busy, rock 'n' roll, seal the deal, shag, plonk, poke, bonk, make the beast with two backs, inter-corpse, pants off-dance off, rock the Casbah, bake the potato, fill the gas tank, churn the butter, stuff the turkey, glaze the donut, release the Kraken.

LIVINGSTON: Really?

DIANE: I don't want you whining all night.

(*DIANE rips the nasal strip off Livingston's nose.*)

LIVINGSTON: I'll draw the curtains.

(*LIVINGSTON steps out of bed. He walks downstage center and looks left and right.*)

LIVINGSTON: We're being watched.

DIANE: What?

(*LIVINGSTON returns to the bed and takes a flashlight out of the bedside table.*)

LIVINGSTON: Come see.

(*She gets out of bed and joins him. They gaze out over the audience.*)

DIANE: Who are they, and what are they doing here?

LIVINGSTON: Probably came to be moved, to be carried away.

DIANE: It's just good to feel anything at all after spending a day at work, anesthetized.

(*LIVINGSTON shines the flashlight over the audience. Stops occasionally on people he finds interesting.*)

LIVINGSTON: It's safer to feel emotions that are shared than those that are felt alone.

(*There's an opportunity for the actors to improvise here as they look out over the audience, commenting on people they might know, on people's clothing. "Look at this one with suspenders!" "This one needs a drink!" And so on. DIANE points to the back row.*)

LIVINGSTON: Is she really asleep?

DIANE: A critic if I ever saw one.

(*A couple seated in the first row, stage right, murmur to each other.*

*LIVINGSTON shines his flashlight on them. The man, FINN, shields his eyes.*)

FINN: You see, that's what I'm talking about. You come to see a romantic comedy, and a bit of absurdist meta-drama breaks out.

ANNA: Shush!

FINN: I won't shush.

ANNA: You're embarrassing me. Everybody's staring at us.

FINN: We should have gone to the movies.

LIVINGSTON: Nobody goes to the movies anymore! Movies are just car chases, shoot-outs, dragons, and boobs.

(*And with that he turns to look at DIANE.*)

ANNA: We're sorry. We'll be good.

DIANE: Finn?

LIVINGSTON: Busted.

(*And with that he turns to look at DIANE.*)

FINN: Hi, Di.

DIANE: Vita's home worried sick about you.

ANNA:
    (*to Finn*)
You told me you had an open marriage.

FINN: Open-ish.

DIANE: And you must be Anne Marie Pollock.

ANNA: Anna Hannah Salmon.

DIANE: The phlebotomist.

ANNA: No.

DIANE: Chiropodist?

ANNA: Dichotomist.

(*LIVINGSTON and DIANE look at each other. He shrugs.*)

DIANE: What do you do?

ANNA: Divide the world into jointly exhaustive and mutually exclusive parts.

LIVINGSTON: Like . . . ?

ANNA: Body and soul.

DIANE: Like those who can, do. Those who can't, teach?

ANNA: Not jointly exhaustive.

LIVINGSTON: There are two kinds of people in the world: those who love to struggle and those who struggle to love.

ANNA: Not mutually exclusive.

DIANE: People who are faithful and people who cheat.

ANNA: The sacred and the profane.

LIVINGSTON: Aren't there any trichotomies?
 (*Pause*)
You know like the sacred, the profane, and the ecstatic.

ANNA: The ecstatic state is a spiritual experience.

LIVINGSTON: Ecstasy is rapturous and pleasurable emotion, isn't it? It's as physical as it gets.
 (*looks at Diane*)
Almost.

FINN: Male, female, transgender.

DIANE: Gender fluid.

LIVINGSTON: Two spirit.

(*MIMI lights up.*)

MIMI: Important Orange Alert. POTUS is missing. He was last seen driving a black and white Club Car golf cart after his seventh shot on the par three 13th hole at Crooked River Golf Club sliced into the woods. 45 was wearing a white polo shirt, khaki trousers, a red ball cap, and orthopedic saddle shoes. If you know anything about 45's whereabouts, please call 911 immediately.

LIVINGSTON: They say he's lost a step.

DIANE: And a marble or two.

LIVINGSTON: His bicycle needs training wheels.

(*Diane's phone plays "By the Sea." She answers.*)

FINN: If it's my wife, I'm not here.

DIANE: Yes. He's here.

ANNA: And I'm out of here!

(*ANNA stands and hurries to the back of the theater and out the door. Others watch, LIVINGSTON, a bit too keenly for Diane's liking.*)

DIANE: Like what you see?

LIVINGSTON: What?

(*DIANE holds the phone out for FINN.*)

DIANE: It's for you.

(*FINN waves off the call. DIANE approaches him and uses the phone to stream a video as FINN smiles and waves to the camera.*)

DIANE
    (*to Vita*)
Yes, we're still on for dinner tomorrow. Six sharp.
    (*Pause*)
I'll hand you over to himself.

(*She hands the phone to FINN.*)

DIANE:
    (*to LIVINGSTON*)
And you! Get dressed!

LIVINGSTON: But you promised.

(*LIVINGSTON sulks and walks toward the coat rack. He gets redressed, shirt, slacks, slippers, as FINN speaks with VITA.*)

FINN: Vita, honey. What a pleasant surprise.
    (*Pause*)
My phone? Dead battery.
    (*Pause*)
I'm with Liv and Di.

(*Pause*)
You thought it looked like a theater on Di's phone?

(*He looks around and then at the phone's screen.*)

FINN: Yes, it does, now that you mention it. Strange.

(*He turns off the camera and his forehead.*)

FINN: Folie a deux.
    (*Pause*)
That's when two people who are close, you and I in this case, share a delusional idea.
    (*Pause*)
That's the only reasonable explanation. The Moodys' bedroom is a theater? Crazy, right?

(*He snaps his fingers to get Livingston's attention.*)

FINN: Vita wants to know if there's a therapist in the house.

(*LIVINGSTON smiles and takes a bow by the coat rack. DIANE looks out over the audience.*)

DIANE: There's got to be a dozen in here if there's one.
    (*Pause*)
Hands up, therapists!

(*She counts of the raised hands, pointing at each in turn.*)

DIANE: Like I said. Hands down!

FINN: Do I love you? Bedefinitely. With all my heart.

DIANE:
    (*to Livingston*)
We only hurt the one we love.
    (*Pause*)

We hurt only the one we love?

LIVINGSTON: We can only betray those who trust us.

FINN: Spur of the moment. I decided to pop in on them.
    (*Pause*)
Well, there are two kinds of people in the world, Vita.
    (*Pause*)
No, not boys and girls. Although that's not incorrect. I mean people who live to love and people who love to live.
    (*Pause*)
You are?
    (*Pause*)
Well, let me ask you, hon. Is what you put into a marriage more important than what you take out of a marriage?
    (*Pause*)
You're breaking up, Vita.
    (*Pause*)
I think I'm losing you.

(*He ends the call and hands the phone back to DIANE.*)

DIANE: Back to your seat.

(*He complies. LIVINGSTON walks toward DIANE as he zips his pants.*)

45 (O.S.): Fore!

(*A golf ball bounces into the bedroom and rolls behind the bed. 45 enters with a golf club, dressed as described by MIMI earlier. He's followed by his caddie [who is played by the actress who played ANNA]. She carries a small golf bag with two clubs, a small bucket of golf balls, wears flats, a party dress, a tiara, and a sash reading "Miss Understood 2019." 45 pokes around searching for his ball. His caddie puts the bucket on the floor.*)

LIVINGSTON: May I help you?

45: I'm playing a Volvik 3.

LIVINGSTON: Is that it behind the bed?

(*45 looks around, nods, kicks the ball out from behind the bed.*)

45: I believe I lie two.

DIANE: Yes, you do. Constantly.

LIVINGSTON
    (*to 45*)
What are you doing?

45: You don't mind if I play through, do you, Chief?

LIVINGSTON: Livingston.

45: Dr. Livingston, I presume.

LIVINGSTON: As a matter of fact . . .

45: That was a historical illusion.

LIVINGSTON: Allusion. Yes, and I've never heard it before.

(*LIVINGSTON notices the caddie and DIANE notices him noticing.*)

LIVINGSTON:
    (*to 45*)
Aren't you going to introduce us?

45: Pardon my manners. My caddie Caddy.
    (*sotto voce*)
A CTS sedan. Luxury trim. Like the chassis?

LIVINGSTON
    (*extends his hand*)

You look familiar.

CADDY: No, I don't.

LIVINGSTON: Liv.

CADDY: Pleased to meet you, I'm sure.

DIANE:
    *(to 45)*
Do you know you're missing?

*(45 touches his face, taps his forehead, turns left, turns right.)*

45: I'm right here. On va-cay.

DIANE: In our bedroom.

45: I've played better courses, I'll have to say.

DIANE: You can't be very good at it if you're in our house.

45: O contrary. I'm tremendous. Everybody says so. I have the stats to prove it. I use many stats.

LIVINGSTON: What's your handicap?

45: I have none.

CADDY: His sons.

*(45 places the ball on a rubber tee in an advantageous spot.)*

45: Casual water.

*(He addresses the ball, takes a few awkward practice swings. As they talk, he appears ready to hit the ball into the audience several times, but each time, he stops to speak.)*

45: And you are?

DIANE: Diane.

LIVINGSTON
   (*to 45*)
We need to get you home.

DIANE: Mimi, call the Secret Service.

MIMI: Calling the sacred cervix.

DIANE
   (*enunciating clearly*)
Se-cret Ser-vice.

MIMI: What about it?

DIANE: Call the Secret Service.

MIMI: Calling the Secret Service.
(*The sound of a ringing phone. The call is answered.*)

VOICE (O.S.): You've reached the Secret Service. All of our agents are busy at this time. Please hold for the next available agent. Your call may be recorded for training and quality assurance.

(*Vacuous music plays softly.*)

(*45 wets his finger and tests the wind. He takes his stance.*)

45: Did I overhear mention of a dinner earlier?

DIANE: We're having friends to dinner tomorrow.
45: At what time?

DIANE: Six.

45: We'll be there fashionably late. What should I bring?

LIVINGSTON: The main course.

45: Is there a McDonald's nearby?

LIVINGSTON: That was a joke. Bring whatever you'd like to drink.

CADDY:
    *(to 45)*
We haven't been invited.

45: We've been asked to bring Diet Coke.

*(45 at last strikes the ball and sends it off into the audience. It's plastic. He shades his eyes to watch the flight.)*

45: I think I'm on the green.

LIVINGSTON: You're in the third row.

45: Mulligan.
    (to Caddy)
Could you grab my balls, sweetheart?

*(He winks at LIVINGSTON. CADDY gives him a ball from the bucket, which he puts down on the tee.)*

LIVINGSTON: Don't let it rile you.

45: I never rile. I have the greatest disposition anyone has. Tremendous disposition.

LIVINGSTON: I suppose it's not if you win or lose, it's how you play the game.

45: It's not how you play the game; it's how you keep score.

DIANE: Where's Melania?

45: Shopping for a jabbar.

(*He mimics a woman putting on a scarf.*)

LIVINGSTON: Do you mean a hijab?

45: I thought it might spice up our cunnbialities.

DIANE: Is that a word?

45: I have all the best words.

LIVINGSTON: Like what?

45: Covfefe.

DIANE: Use it in a sentence.

45: Ask your doctor if covfefe is right for you.

(*As he strikes the ball, the music stops, the lights go down. MIMI lights up.*)

[Note: 45 pronounces this nonce word co-fef-ee.]

MIMI: I've been disconnected.

(*Dial tone.*)

## ACT II

*(Stage is dark. House lights are up. The crew is putting final touches on the new set. Lobby lights flash, announcing the end of intermission. As the audience drifts back to their seats, MIMI, on her table, lights up and begins.)*

MIMI: Pardon our disarray as we arrange the set for Act II, "Guess Who's Coming to Dinner?" This morning Di called her lawyer, Eddie Shamgochian, and set the wheels of her divorce in motion.
*(Pause)*
Meanwhile, across town at the Trump lodgings . . .

*(45 and CADDY cross the stage right to left. n their way, 45 spritzes his hair with a cloud of aerosol spray. CADDY follows and coughs, covers her mouth and nose.)*

45: I want to use hairspray, but they say, Don't use hairspray. It's bad for the ozone. So I'm in a concealed apartment, this concealed unit. I don't think anything gets out, and I'm not supposed to be using hairspray?

CADDY: Do you mean sealed unit, sir?

*(CADDY holds up a hand mirror. 45 inspects his do.)*

45: The worst thing a man can do in his life is to go bald.

*(They exit left.)*

MIMI:
*(Coughs)*
The guests are dining now in the kitchen. Oh, and before I forget, please turn off all personal electronic devices, including laptops and cell phones. Smoking is prohibited for the duration of the play. Thank you so much.

(*House lights are down, stage lights up. The bed is now a couch, the storage chest a coffee table, the night tables are end tables, a small lamp on each. Mimi's on the left table as is Liv's Einstein book. The vanity is now a bar. The cafe table and two chairs remain. A comfy chair at either side of the couch. The door at left leads to the kitchen, at right, to the bathroom.*)

MIMI: And now that you're settled, Di enters from left

(*DIANE walks to the bar, pours herself a drink, and turns to address the audience.*)

DIANE: Marriage is a closed system that evolves toward a state of maximum entropy, decline, degeneration, irreversible dissipation, and collapse.
    (*Pause*)
The way that ice melts to water, wood burns to ash, smoke, and gas.
    (*Pause*)
I don't want us to be one of those couples who stay married, drift into deceit, hostility, and indifference.
    (*Pause*)
Indifference is the opposite of love. Marriage is the opposite of new.
    (*Pause*)
Entropy always wins, but we can hold it off for a while.
    (*Pause*)
You're no doubt wondering about our little dinner party. Well, Liv is lactose intolerant; Finn has celiac disease; Caddy is vegan, and Vita is allergic to shellfish. So I made soy-free, nut-free, gluten-free, vegan friendly mac 'n' dairy-free coconut oil-based bio-cheese black bean burgers, hold the buns. No animals were harmed or even touched in the making of the meal. 45 brought his own bucket of grub.

(*As LIVINGSTON ushers CADDY and 45 into the living room, DIANE exits, drink in hand, to the kitchen. 45 wears a white shirt, blue suit, long red tie. He removes a napkin from the collar of his shirt. They*

*head for the bar.)*
LIVINGSTON: May I offer you a drink?

45: I've never had a drop of alcohol in my life.

CADDY: I'll have a negroni.

45: Lips that touch liquor shall never touch mine.

CADDY: Make it a double.

LIVINGSTON
    *(to 45)*
What else have you never done in your life?

45 : I've never apologized. I've never vacuumed a carpet or fed a baby. I've never taken a mulligan.

CADDY: You did yesterday.

45: Never did. Never blown up a balloon, polished silverware, made a bed, folded laundry, shined shoes, shopped at a supermarket, never cheated in a Business Ethics class at Wharton, or separated children from their parents.

CADDY: Actually, you did do that. April 2018.

45: Never did. Crooked Hillary.

CADDY: Look me in the eye and say that.

*(He looks her in the eye.)*

45: I was lifting weights with Squee that night. Just ask PJ or Torbin.
    *(Pause)*
I've never doubted anything I've ever said.

LIVINGSTON: Well, logically, if someone doubts something, we know they must have at least thought about it.

45: Sad.

(*As LIVINGSTON mixes Caddy's drink, 45 notices the Einstein book on the end table, picks it up, and examines it.*)

45: Any relation to Harvey?

LIVINGSTON: Einstein, not Weinstein. An immigrant, by the way.

45: I've heard the name plenty of times. "Nice job, Einstein!"
 (*Pause*)
Must have been a klutz, right?

LIVINGSTON: A genius.

45: I have a very large, eh, brain.

LIVINGSTON: Compared to what?

(*LIVINGSTON hands CADDY her drink, picks up his own, CADDY takes a seat on the couch.*)

45: My IQ is one of the highest ever.

LIVINGSTON: How high?

45: Don't feel stupid or insecure. It's not your fault.

LIVINGSTON: Give me a number. Ball park. How high?

45: Almost a hundred. Let's just say you could round it off to a hundred.
 (*Pause*)

Perfect score.

(*DIANE enters with VITA and FINN. VITA holds her dog Bullet, a plush toy, in one arm.*)

45: So what do you people do when you get together?

(*He pulls a burger out of his jacket pocket, unwraps it, and takes a bite.*)

DIANE: We people?

45: You salt-of-the-earth types.

LIVINGSTON: We talk about the weather.

45: That hurricane we had last fall was something. The wettest we've ever had in terms of rain.

VITA: Climate change.

45: No such thing. Fake news.

VITA: Ninety-nine percent of scientists say it is true.

45: The Chinese started it to ruin the American economy.

FINN: We play charades.

VITA: Guys versus gals.

45: Shirts versus skins.

FINN: We're first.

(*FINN takes a card off the end table, reads it, puts it down, and mimes opening a book.*)

LIVINGSTON: Book title!

45: The Bible!
(FINN *shakes his head and mimes painting a picture. 45 copies the gesture with a puzzled look on his face.*)

LIVINGSTON: Art. The art. The art of.

(FINN's *driving a car. Tugs his ear.*)

LIVINGSTON: Sounds like.

(FINN *turns the steering wheel, points at it. Again, 45 makes the same movements.*)

45: Chauffeur.

LIVINGSTON: Sounds like wheel. The Art of the ... Deal.

(FINN *indicates the winning response. All cheer.*)

45: The Art of the Steal?

FINN
    (*to 45*)
Deal! How did you not get that?

45: Bad clues.

FINN: You wrote it.

45: But I didn't read it.
    (*Pause*)
Who knew reading would be so hard.

LIVINGSTON: What have you read?

45: The Bible, of course.

FINN: What's your favorite part?

45: The Book of Hesitations. When the dinosaurs enter Jerusalem and Hercules has to save the city with the help of the angels, and those two Corinthians walk into a bar.

DIANE: Do you think you'll write another book?

45: We all learn to write when we're five, but some of us get over it. I wrote a poem in high school. Did you know I was a great baseball player?

DIANE: I did not.

45: I like to hear the crowd give cheers, / So loud and noisy to my ears. / When the score is 5-5, / I feel like I could cry. / And when they get another run, / I feel like I could die. / Then the catcher makes an error,/ Not a bit like Yogi Berra. / The game is over and we say? Tomorrow is another day.

(*45 takes a bow.*)

45: I got the constellation prize for that. I was a star.

(*DIANE taps a spoon against her glass, calling for attention.*)

DIANE: Liv and I have an announcement to make.

(*DIANE smiles, walks downstage left, and holds out her hand. LIVINGSTON joins her; they clasp hands and face their guests, from stage right to left: CADDY, in a comfy chair, FINN and VITA on the couch, and 45, in a comfy chair.*)

DIANE: Liv and I are giving ourselves a second chance.

LIVINGSTON: We're getting a divorce.

(*DIANE and LIVINGSTON smile at each other; FINN and VITA look dismayed and confused. 45 tweets on his phone. CADDY sips her drink and perks up.*)
45: Did you have a pre-nup?

(*LIVINGSTON and DIANE shake their heads.*)

45: Then you'll need a post-nup.
    (*Pause*)
Did you have beautiful babies?

LIVINGSTON: No.

DIANE: Poppy.

(*She pulls out her phone and shows 45 a photo.*)

LIVINGSTON: She got it off a website. Thispersondoesnotexist.com.

45: I've got four beautiful kids.

VITA: You've got five.

45: Junior and Erik, Ivanka,
    (*Moans*)
Barron, and the other one.

DIANE: I feel like a great weight has been lifted from my shoulders.

LIVINGSTON: We believe it's the right thing to do.

(*FINN turns and smiles at CADDY, gets his flirty eyebrows going. VITA hugs Bullet tightly.*)

DIANE: We are still very much in love.

LIVINGSTON: Even more so today than yesterday, knowing what we almost lost.

DIANE: We knew it was time to act in an unhabitual way.

LIVINGSTON: Every end is a beginning.

DIANE: Our redemption.

LIVINGSTON: Our second act.

DIANE: A divorce, mind you, not a separation. We are not dedomiciling or disuniting.

LIVINGSTON: We're staying together.

VITA: So nothing changes.

DIANE: Everything changes.

VITA: You'll still be together.

LIVINGSTON: Because we want to be, not because we have to be. We're going back in time to pre-marital bliss.

*(A cell phone activates in the audience. The ringtone is a male voice singing "Stormy." That gets 45's attention. An embarrassed MAN fumbles for his phone. The actors freeze and turn. The ringtone continues at a lower volume.)*

MAN: Sorry! So sorry! I'm a doctor. On call. Emergency. Sorry.

DIANE: Well, answer it!

MAN: I lied. I'm not a doctor. It's my wife. She's pregnant.

DIANE: Answer it!

MAN: She's not pregnant, actually. She's needy.

DIANE: Could you please--
(*The MAN holds up a finger silencing DIANE.*)

MAN: Yes, dear. Milk and what else?
    (*Pause*)
What exactly is Brazilian Bum Bum Cream?
    (*Pause*)
Oh!

DIANE: Could you please take it out to the lobby please!

MAN: Wives, you can't live with them, you can't . . .

(*He withers and stops talking when all the women on stage take one step in his direction and stare him down, daring him to continue. With the phone to his ear, he heads for the lobby.*)

MAN: I'm at a play.
    (*Pause*)
No, I'm not gay, sweetheart. Play.
    (*Pause*)
It's not the same.

DIANE
    (*to the women*)
There's a seat for every ass.

45: What you need is a wall here. I can build you a great wall. Mexico will pay for it.

LIVINGSTON: It is a wall, the fourth wall. It's a conceptual barrier, not a physical barrier, a shared metaphor between the actors and the audience.

FINN: Places!

LIVINGSTON: Where were we? We're divorced because we want to be.

DIANE: Close enough.
    (*to audience*)
We do apologize.

(*The actors variously clear their throats, roll their necks and shoulders, hop up and down, recite tongue twisters, and otherwise prepare to get back into character and soldier on.*)

ALL:
    (*speaking at once*)
Gooda gooda Buddha Buddha! Unique New York! She sells seashells by the seashore! How can a clam cram in a clean cream can?

(*They hit their marks. VITA sits with Bullet on her lap.*)

LIVINGSTON: Love is an emotion.

DIANE: A behavior.

FINN: Love is an algorithm.

VITA: But troubled love is a story.

LIVINGSTON: An emotion and a behavior.

DIANE: Affection, tenderness, and solicitous attention.

LIVINGSTON: Marriage, on the other hand, is an institution. I'm not ready to spend any more time in an institution.

DIANE: We'll still be in love, just not married.

VITA: You're fooling yourself. Aren't you just running away from your problem, Di?

DIANE: There is no growth without change, Vita. That is why we do things that we are afraid to do. We take risks; we don't settle or stagnate.

LIVINGSTON: And nothing will need to be divided, sold, replaced. We can have the same banal conversations we've always had.

DIANE: Did you take out the garbage, dear?

LIVINGSTON: I will as soon as I finish this chapter.

DIANE: Never mind, I'll do it.

LIVINGSTON: That kind of conversation.

VITA
    (*to Diane*)
Didn't you tell me just yesterday that Finn and I should stay together and work out our issues?

LIVINGSTON: It's a meat and poison situation.

(*FINN is making eyes at CADDY.*)

VITA: What does that mean?

LIVINGSTON: One man's meat is another man's poison.

45: One man's profit is another man's loss.

FINN: One man's pleasure is another man's pain.

CADDY: It's always about the man, isn't it?

VITA: I think both of you are being pretty cavalier about this.
 (*Pause*)
We marry for love.

FINN: We marry because we don't want to be alone.

VITA: They've got a pill for that.

LIVINGSTON: We want to be cared for.

DIANE: We need to care for someone.

VITA: That's what pets are for.

(*She pats Bullet and sees FINN flirting with CADDY.*)

VITA: What are you doing?

FINN: Nothing.

LIVINGSTON: He's canoodling.

45: Not canoodling.

VITA
 (*to Finn*)
Canoodle no more!

(*CADDY stands and walks to the bar where she will pour herself a drink. Finn's eyes follow her.*)

DIANE: Finn makes it interesting for you, doesn't he? Keeps you on your toes.

VITA: Even when I'd rather be on my back.

45: Canoodling is not a crime.

VITA: Marriage is our culture's great statement of optimism. Love abides; until death do us part.
   (*Pause*)
If you fail at marriage, you fail at the most important relationship in your life.
   (*Pause*)
Can I get an Amen?
(*She glares at FINN.*)

FINN: Amen.

VITA: Finn and I will not fail. Will we, dear?

FINN: Amen.

VITA: I love Finn.

DIANE: I love Liv.

45: I love a mystery.

DIANE: Love is what keeps you from dying.

LIVINGSTON: Nothing does that.

DIANE: While you're alive, I mean.

VITA: We begin marriage counseling tomorrow.

DIANE: That's wonderful, Vita.

(*DIANE embraces VITA. 45 pulls a can of Diet Coke out of his pocket and pops the tab--very loudly. Raises the can.*)

45: Here's to Vita and Finn!

(*They all toast VITA and FINN.*)

FINN: And here's to Liv and Di.

(*They all raise their glasses.*)

DIANE: As soon as the divorce is final, Liv and I are taking a second honeymoon in ...
(*They speak simultaneously.*)

DIANE: Paris!

LIVINGSTON: Vegas!

DIANE: We're still working out the details.

45: The first month of divorce is the sweetest.

LIVINGSTON: Does our conversation tonight remind anyone else of Plato's Symposium?

(*Apparently not.*)

LIVINGSTON: Our discussion?

CADDY: I don't think there were any ladies present at that banquet.

LIVINGSTON: True enough.

CADDY: A bunch of philosophers sitting around talking about the great and glorious god Love.

LIVINGSTON: We may not be philosophers, but this is what we talk about when we talk about love.

VITA: And marriage.

LIVINGSTON: Yes.

DIANE: And divorce.

LIVINGSTON: Shall we continue our symposium?

45: I'll be what's-his-name.

LIVINGSTON: Socrates?

45: Right!

LIVINGSTON: You'll ask questions.

45: Wrong! I'm an answer man. I'm an expert on marriage.

(*MIMI lights up.*)

DIANE: You've been married three times.

45: I rest my case.

DIANE: So why three marriages?

45: Wives are like cars. Every so often you have to trade up to a classier model.

LIVINGSTON: Women aren't commodities. I think that's insulting.

DIANE: Me too!

VITA: Me too!

CADDY: Me too!

MIMI: Important Orange Alert. POTUS is still missed, no not missed, missing. He was last seen leaving the Amour Motel in

Shrewsbury with his caddie and their driver. POTUS was wearing a blue suit, white shirt, red tie, and black Giocometti calfskin leather orthopedic oxfords. If you see him, please ask him to call Robert Mueller immediately.

45: Slippery Bob. Witch hunt. No collusion, Crooked Hillary. Not a puppet. He can call me.

(*He stands, addresses an imaginary golf ball, and takes a swing.*)

45: On the green in regulation.

CADDY: Your number's unlisted.

(*He sets up for a putt. CADDY mimes holding the flag.*)

45: A lot of golfers are switching to these really long putters-- very unattractive, weird. Some great people use them. Really long putters. I hate that. I'm a traditionalist.

DIANE: What are you talking about?

45: Gay marriage.

DIANE: Not your short putter?

(*Indicates his crotch.*)

45: Believe me there are no complaints about the commander-in-chief.

FINN: You think gay marriage is a fad?

45: I have many fabulous friends who happen to be gay through no fault of their own. But me, I'm a traditionalist.
  (*Pause*)
The gays love me.

FINN: No, they don't.

45: I've done more for gays than any president in history.

FINN: No, you haven't.

45: Fake news.

VITA: Boys, that's quite enough.
    *(Pause)*
Bullet needs some water. Don't you, baby? Yes, you do.

(*VITA digs a water bowl out of her purse, sets Bullet down on the couch, and exits to the kitchen.*)

45
    (*to Livingston*)
The men's room?

(*LIVINGSTON points to the door. 45 digs his phone out of his pocket and exits through the door.*)

FINN
    (*to Caddy*)
What's it like working for the boss?

CADDY: He's not such a bad guy, you know. It's all a show to him. He feels compelled to play the role his base expects him to.

DIANE: Base is the right word.

LIVINGSTON: I suppose he's on his best behavior tonight, but we all see him at his worst all day, every day. He's a surly, petulant, narcissistic, delusional, ignorant, bullying racist predator.

(*45 enters while tweeting.*)

45: You rang?

(*Finishes the tweet and puts the phone in his pocket.*)

45: That's it then. We're pulling out of Antarctica. Stat.
   (*Pause*)
It was an anomonous decision.

LIVINGSTON: Do you mean unanimous?

45: We all agreed and nobody knows who we are.
   (*Pause*)
It's an unpresidented move.

LIVINGSTON: Do you mean unprecedented?

45: Grammar Nazi.

(*The doorbell rings.*)

DIANE: Don't you love the chime of a doorbell? It's always a mystery. Could be anybody. It might be danger. Or the Publishers' Clearinghouse Sweepstakes. Or a process server.

(*A knock at the door.*)

DIANE: It could be opportunity.

(*A knock at the door.*)

LIVINGSTON: Opportunity only knocks once.

VITA (O.S.): I've got it.

(*CADDY uses a napkin to wipe 45's chin.*)

CADDY: You're drooling, sir.

(*VITA appears at the door, bowl in hand.*)

VITA: She says her name is Mary Faford.

(*DIANE stares daggers at LIVINGSTON.*)

DIANE:
> (*to Livingston*)
What is she doing here?

LIVINGSTON: Perhaps I should speak with her.

DIANE: You stay right where you are.

VITA: She says Liv left his credit card at the store.

DIANE: And she thought she'd return it in person.

VITA: I sent her on her way.

DIANE:
> (*to Livingston*)
This is not an open divorce. Is that what you think it is?

(*VITA holds up the card, hands it to LIVINGSTON, sets both the bowl and Bullet on the floor by the couch.*)

DIANE: You're free from the marriage but not from me.

45: She's playing the woman card.

VITA: This divorce is not getting off to a good start. Perhaps, you should reconsider and join Finn and me in counseling.

(*FINN flirts with CADDY.*)

VITA: Right, Finn?
>(*Pause*)
Are you even listening?

FINN: I am.

VITA: What did I say?

FINN: The usual.

(*Three conversations proceed at the same time. We listen to bits of each. FINN and CADDY: she sits on the chair at right, FINN on the couch beside her. DIANE and VITA on the couch and chair respectively, at left. LIVINGSTON and 45 sit at the table downstage.*)

LIVINGSTON: And then you made grotesque fun of a man's disability in public. Who does that?

45: It was an homage.

FINN: What's your sign?

CADDY: For Sale. What's yours?

(*DIANE and VITA look at their husbands and speak in unison.*)

DIANE AND VITA: Maybe I'm making a big mistake.

(*They smile and link pinkies.*)

DIANE AND VITA: Jinx!

FINN: I'm a Leo. I'm told I'm irresistible.

CADDY:
>(*Leans back*)
Then there must be some anti-gravity in the room.

VITA: He thinks he's God's gift to women.

LIVINGSTON: Could you not text while we're talking. Please and thank you.

DIANE: I like him more than I like us.

CADDY: I got a text.

FINN: Read it.
CADDY:
    (*Looks at 45, reads.*)
Call our driver.

    (*Makes the call.*)
ASAP.

45: Do you ever lie?

LIVINGSTON: For a living.

45: Journalist?

FINN: Uber or Lyft?

CADDY: Chauffeur.

LIVINGSTON: I call it giving people hope.

45: That's what I call it, too. Politician?

VITA: Maybe I should just let him go.

FINN: Pie or cake?

DIANE: He doesn't want to go. He wants you and a little on the side.

VITA: He can't have his cake and eat it too.

CADDY: Ice cream.

LIVINGSTON: Therapist.

45: I don't believe you.

LIVINGSTON: Does that make you angry?

DIANE: You can't swim and not get wet.

FINN: Beatles or Stones?

DIANE: The more we change, the more we stay the same.

CADDY: Who?

VITA: How does that make you feel?

FINN: Sad.

DIANE: Sad.

45: Sad.

LIVINGSTON: Do you want to go with that feeling?

45: Go where?
    (*Pause*)
We used to have a great country, founded on life, liberty, and the pursuit of happiness.

LIVINGSTON: Just to be clear, it was founded on genocide and slavery.

45: On the rule of law.

LIVINGSTON: That protects the one percent.

45: From the immigrants. The brown-skins.

DIANE: Your mother was an immigrant. Your grandfather was an immigrant. Two of your wives were immigrants.

LIVINGSTON:
 (*to 45*)
That's pretty insulting, don't you think?
45: I was blessed with a tiny conscience.

DIANE: What about your legacy?

45: I'm not concerned with what happens after I die.
 (*Pause*)
I wanted to make America great again.

DIANE: It has never been great for a great many people.

45: And yet we believe it was. A good story always trumps the truth.

LIVINGSTON: Where is the justice?

45: It's not about justice. It's about order. Law and order, not law and justice. Justice is a luxury. It's not about equality either. We all want to be better than the next guy, Why settle for equality? Equality is for losers.

(*45 turns to the audience and walks to downstage center; LIVINGSTON joins VITA and DIANE. 45 is more subdued here than is usual, but all the signature gestures are there: accordion hands, finger circle, upward gun, L-shape and pinch, etc.*)

45: I'm not who they say I am. I'm hinged. Totally hinged. Not

surly or petulant or bombastic. Not a liar. Not a puppet. Not a crook. Yes, the name-calling hurts. The belittling hurts. I'm a successful businessman, a stable genius, the leader of the free world.
  (*Pause*)
Americans would never elect a sexual predator as president, a con man who's been sued 3500 times, a flagrant liar, a malicious bully. Fake news. Who you going to believe, me or the failing T & G?
  (*Pause*)
Don't I deserve compassion, even if I say I don't want it? You don't know my suffering. You have no idea what battles are going on down there in my soul. You don't think I bleed?
  (*Pause*)
I had beautiful pictures taken in which I had a big smile on my face. I looked happy, content. I looked like a very nice person, which, in theory, is what I am. I'm actually a nice person. I have a great temperament. My temperament is very strong, very calm.
  (*Pause*)
I've sometimes said the wrong things--my caustic campaign language. I regret causing anyone any personal pain. Sometimes I'm just too honest. Sure, I cheat on my wife. I provoke violence, but I'm still a good guy.
  (*Pause*)
No one respects women more than me. I'm the least racist person you've ever met. I build the best walls and the best buildings. Maybe I like myself too much, but I made a tremendous difference in this country. Everybody says so. Thank god for 45, they say. Thank god for me. Me!

(MIMI *lights up.*)

45: Mimi, play "The Beauty of Me."

(*The music begins. 45 sings the verses, the others sing the chorus.*)

[Note: Button and Nipple are 45's mispronunciations of Bhutan and Nepal. In the last line, sung by all, 45 uses the first person.

To the tune of Gilbert and Sullivan's "When I Was a Lad."]

MIMI: Playing "The Beauty of Me," live at the Worcester County Light Opera Company.

45: I celebrate myself and I sing myself,
And I keep my Emmy on the mantel shelf.
I'm a doting daddy so it's no surprise
I keep Ivanka's photo with my Nobel Prize.

CHORUS: He doesn't have an Emmy or a Nobel Prize,
But he does have an ego that is bigly sized.
45: When I was a lad, I worked for my dad,
The real estate biz was my launching pad.
Flown to Button and to Nipple and one of the 'istans,
And I settled our dispute with little Rocket Man.

CHORUS: He's solid, he's sound, he has no regrets,
Spends his executive time on the Internets.

45: I served my country in military school,
My number of infractions was minuscule.
I would have been a general in Vietnam,
But a devastating heel spur foiled my plan.

CHORUS: When he's at center stage or he's lying low
He's not Putin's puppet, he's Pinocchio.

45: They call me Agent Orange and an arrant knave,
What the snobs say is heartless, I say is brave,
When I want to talk to the man on the street,
I retire to my throne and I tweet tweet tweet.

CHORUS: In his little room on his porcelain seat
Is where he composes his Presidential Suite.

45: I don't pay taxes and that means I'm smart

And I pay no attention to the bleeding hearts.
Speak power to truth I always say.
And now I am the ruler of the USA.

CHORUS: And now he is the ruler of the USA?
His diplomatic prowess ever on display.

45: My brain is wider than the sky.
I'm a matinee idol you can't deny.
When I want to charm, I just hit the switch
The beauty of me is I'm mega rich.

CHORUS: He's mega rich and wears a MAGA hat;
He's got little fingers and a little fat.
By any measure he's gone astray,

ALL: But now he is the ruler of the USA.

(*As the song ends, the doorbell chimes three times.*)

DIANE: Avon calling! ... calling! ... calling!

LIVINGSTON: We've got company!

FINN: Someone order pizza?

(*VITA sits on the couch. Bullet yips and barks. She lifts him to her lap.*)

VITA: It's okay, baby. Mommy's here.

45: Must be Rudy.

CADDY: Our driver. I'll let him in.

(*She exits through the kitchen.*)

45: Glad I could help out with the marital issues.

(*He points to each one he addresses in turn.*)

45:
    (*to Diane*)
Use your leverage.
    (*to Livingston*)
Fight back.
    (*to Finn*)
Have fun.
    (*to Vita*)
Deliver the goods.

(*CADDY enters with RUDY. He's played by the actor last seen answering his phone in the audience. He takes off his chauffeur's cap. He's bald, bespectacled, bug-eyed, and sweating. He wears a red clown nose, which he removes and puts in his jacket pocket.*)

FINN: You look familiar.

RUDY: I'm not.

VITA: I know you. You're his lawyer.

RUDY: No lawyer. No longer.

FINN: You're a chauffeur now?

RUDY: I'm a knight of the empire.

FINN: In World of Warcraft?

RUDY: The presidential vindicator. The adjutant of insult.

(*Rudy's phone plays "Stormy." Puzzled, FINN looks at the audience. RUDY takes the clown nose out of his pocket, puts it back, and takes out his phone.*)

RUDY
> (*Whispers*)
Secret Service.

(*He doesn't answer, re-pockets the silenced phone.*)

VITA: We've been talking about love and marriage and divorce tonight. I know you've been married three times. Maybe you could give us some advice.

RUDY: Twice.

VITA: No, three times. That's a fact.

RUDY: Facts are in the eye of the beholder.

LIVINGSTON: No, they're not. You're thinking of beauty.

VITA: I can Google it.

(*She takes out her phone and types.*)

RUDY: Look it! There are factoids, facts, true facts, facsimiles, facticities, factions, and factors.
> (*Pause*)
Follow me? It's confusing mess. Chaos.

LIVINGSTON: That's why we gave fact-checkers. They look for the truth.

RUDY: Truth isn't truth.

(*RUDY's perspiring mightily. He takes out a Yankees hanky, snaps it open, and blots his face and bald head.*)

RUDY: There's the truth as you see it.

45: And there's the truth the people want to hear.

VITA
    (*Reads her phone.*)
First you married your cousin--

RUDY: It was annulled.

VITA: After fourteen years.

RUDY: Never happened. Ask the Pope. Two marriages.

VITA: Three.

RUDY: As we say in Brooklyn, Nyet!
CADDY: We should be going.
    (*to Diane*)
Thank you so much for your hospitality.

FINN
    (*to 45*)
Do you have any last words for us on marriage?

45: One thing I have learned. There is high maintenance. There is low maintenance. I want no maintenance.

(*RUDY, CADDY, and 45 exit through the kitchen. LIVINGSTON follows.*)

RUDY (O.S.): It's snowing.

CADDY (O.S.): It's June.

RUDY (O.S.): What is falling then?

45 (O.S.): Nothing to worry about.

(*LIVINGSTON returns to the room, brushing what looks like ash from his hair and holding on to three party hats.*)

VITA: We should go.

LIVINGSTON: You'll want a hat.

(*He hands the hats to VITA and FINN, puts on his own. They put theirs on.*)

FINN: Party's over.

LIVINGSTON: I'll drive you home.

(*Hugs and kisses. LIVINGSTON, VITA, and FINN exit through the kitchen. DIANE takes a chair from the table, walks downstage center, and sits.*)
DIANE: You can be adventurous in your life. You can follow your bliss, as they say. You can explore the glorious world around you. Or you can affix yourself to a place or a condition and hang on like a sea squirt, a saclike marine filter-feeding hermaphrodite--no need to find a date to have some fun--and attach yourself to a rock where you will spend the rest of your days. Till death do you part. First thing you do is eat your brain because you don't need that anymore. True fact, as they say. Eat your backbone 'cause you ain't going nowhere. Eat your eye. Who needs it now? Life is not a journey for you.
    (*Pause*)
I met Liv at the Stop & Shop where I worked after school in the meat department. He stocked shelves. I was talking to my manager Bob Farrell when Liv butts in without an apology to ask Bob for a ride home and walks away without a glance in my direction. It was love at first slight. Those bedroom eyes, that dreamy smile.

(*She shuts her eyes, rolls her neck, smiles, and then gathers herself.*)

DIANE: We flirted at the store's Christmas party. We went to his senior prom at Wachusett Country Club. While the Coyotes kept everyone on the dance floor, Liv and I snuck away and

walked across the golf course until we could barely hear the music. We found ourselves on the fourteenth green where we got out of our clothes and into each other. And then all the sprinklers turned on, so we ran around naked, slipping and sliding on the grass until we heard the siren and saw the flashing lights. We grabbed the gown, the rented tux, the shoes, and ran off into the woods.
    *(Pause)*
And that right there was the only moment in my life you could write a song about.

*(She dances her way to the bar and pours herself a drink.)*

DIANE: We got engaged. I countered his college infidelities with my own tepid affair with Wendell Mattress, Realtor, whose slogan was "I know where you live," which he thought was funny, but I thought was disturbing. Of course, I was cheating on Wendell with Liv. Wendell was one of those emotionally self-sustaining guys who tolerate, but don't need, anyone else. So it was not a problem when I re-engaged with Liv. We took the next logical step and got married.

*(She puts the drink down, opens her phone and looks at the photo of Poppy. She returns to her seat.)*

DIANE: When I got pregnant, we persuaded ourselves we weren't quite ready for the responsibilities of parenthood. Another year or two, we lied. Plenty of time later, we said. I had the procedure done.
    *(Pause)*
I was unable to conceive after that. Finn and Vita think that not having kids is virtuous--saving the planet with a smaller carbon footprint.
    *(To the photo)*
Poppy.
    *(Pause)*
Are we defined by what's missing in our lives?

*(She takes a deep, restorative breath.)*

DIANE: When Liv and I were young, we burned so hot we were consumed by the passion that we were nourished by. And here we stand in the ashes.
   *(Pause)*
Ashes to ashes, dust to dust.
   *(Pause)*
Everything's broken. Everyone hurts. That's how it feels some days.

*(LIVINGSTON enters in party hat.)*

LIVINGSTON: Who are you talking to?

*(DIANE turns off the phone and pockets it.)*

LIVINGSTON: And don't say *Poppy*.

DIANE: Not Poppy.

LIVINGSTON: You know I don't like that.

*(He pulls up a chair beside her and takes a seat.)*

DIANE: What are we doing?

LIVINGSTON: You're punishing yourself for no reason.

DIANE: It's hard to live up to your youthful passion.

LIVINGSTON: And unnecessary. We're not youthful anymore. Maybe we should be putting on the brakes.

DIANE: We're at a dead stop. We have to keep moving or we'll die.
   *(Pause)*

You know, like whale sharks.
>    (*Pause*)

We don't need to go fast. We don't need to go far. But we need to move.
>    (*Pause*)

I feel dull, dreary, deflated. Ordinary. I'd rather be on fire than be ordinary.

LIVINGSTON: The divorce is a stupid idea.

DIANE: I know that.

LIVINGSTON: What were we thinking of?

DIANE: I was afraid that we'll miss this opportunity--maybe our last opportunity--to turn the page and start a new chapter.
>    (*Pause*)

Regret eats the soul.
>    (*Pause*)

I don't want to know how our story ends--

LIVINGSTON: There's only one ending.

DIANE: I want to follow the rising action, the twists and turns of the plot--there has to be a plot or else we've flat-lined. I want to be surprised. That's what gets me up in the morning--wondering what's going to happen next. If I already know, if it's more of the same, I might as well stay in bed. I want discovery, adventure, promise, change.

LIVINGSTON: There's something to be said for routine and habit.

DIANE: Not much,

LIVINGSTON: Security--

DIANE: Give me uncertainty and expectation.

LIVINGSTON: Comfort, solace. A marriage is a sanctuary.

DIANE: Another word for asylum. I'm not crazy. I'm just a little cracked.

LIVINGSTON: And who's going to put up with us but us?

(*The doorbell chimes. The door opens. The sounds of people tromping in. LIVINGSTON and DIANE stand and turn.*)

RUDY (O.S.) : Excessive concern with little weasels is a sickness. Get help!


(*45 enters followed by RUDY, hatless and wearing sunglasses. Rudy's hand is on 45's shoulder. CADDY walks past them into the room. She carries a children's black doctor's bag.*)

DIANE: What happened?

RUDY: Fairness please!

CADDY: We had a little accident.

RUDY: Supervision please!

45: Rudy was driving in the breakdown lane and he had one. A nervous one. Blew a fuse.

(*RUDY walks away from 45 and feels his way around the room.*)

CADDY: He lost control of the golf cart, went up over the sidewalk and into a tree.

45: He was screaming about disposable men and muscle guys

and ferrets, and the veins on his forehead bubbled out. When he hit the tree with tremendous impact, his eyes popped right out of his head and bounced off the dashboard.

(RUDY *drifts downstage and sings quietly behind the conversation. CADDY keeps an eye on him. 45 sits on the sofa.*)

RUDY
    (*Sings*)
Nobody knows the trouble I've seen.

CADDY: Those were golf balls. But he has suffered some fleeting blindness and will need some attention.

DIANE: I'm a nurse.

LIVINGSTON: I'm a therapist.
CADDY: I'm a doctor.

(*She holds up the bag.*)

45: I'm a scratch golfer.

CADDY: I've given him aspirin, checked his vitals. I called the paramedics. On their way.

RUDY
    (*Sings*)
Sometimes I'm up, sometimes I'm down.

(RUDY's *about to walk off the stage when* CADDY *grabs him.*)

CADDY: You've gone too far.

RUDY: So they tell me.

CADDY: Come with me.

(*She leads him to the sofa.*)

RUDY: A wall is not a wall.

(*CADDY sits RUDY down beside 45. She sits in the chair beside them. RUDY lays his head on 45's chest, and 45 Puts a comforting arm around him.*)

RUDY: I lied for you.

45: Many times. Not a rat. You gave up your reputation for me. Hero to zero.
    (*Pause*)
And I don't know why.

RUDY: There's no collusion.

45: Who does that?

RUDY: I never said there was no collusion.

CADDY: A friend does that.

45: I must have a lot of friends.

RUDY: Show me where it says collusion is a crime.

45: There's no one else here, right?

(*LIVINGSTON and DIANE turn to the audience and turn back.*)

LIVINGSTON: No.

DIANE: Ain't nobody here but us chickens.

45: Let me speak frankly.
    (*Pause*)

Yes, I have investments in Russia. Yes, I get funding from Russia. Cohen, Stone, Junior, Jared, Ivanka, yada, yada, yada, they all met with Russian officials.
   (*Pause*)
Those are the facts, but most people are not interested in facts.

CADDY: There is a darkness in all of us.

RUDY: Let a light shine in the darkness.

CADDY: Anger, fear, insecurity, our pain, our jealousies, our regrets, our helplessness.
   (*Pause*)
Most of us avoid the darkness, but that's where he goes. He goes to our darkness and mines it.

45: When I said I could shoot a man on Fifth Avenue and not lose voters, I was right. Hard to believe. My unwavering base. (*45 Takes his arm off Rudy's shoulder. The arm has gone numb and dangles at his side. He stands.*)

45: It's a simple matter to drag the people along. I know more about people than anyone.
   (*Pause*)
Tell them they're under attack and they'll do what you want.
   (*Pause*)
Who said that?

LIVINGSTON: Hermann Goering.

45: They know nothing, but they don't know they know nothing, so I can tell them anything.

DIANE: That's a cynical view of your supporters.

45: They want someone who will tell them what to do. I'm their man.

RUDY: Freedom is about submission to authority.

45: A stern and confident father who can be aggressive if need be. They want affirmation, not so-called truth. They want assurance that their fears are real. They feel imperiled, and I keep pointing out the threats.
 *(Pause)*
Does that make me a bad guy?

*(He collapses back on the sofa.)*

CADDY: He's not heartless, but he thinks a display of tenderness will leave him open to assault.

LIVINGSTON: Are you saying there's hope for the old guy yet?

CADDY: If he can embrace his vulnerability, then think of the good he could do.

DIANE: Let's not get carried away.

LIVINGSTON: He seems to be lacking in compassion.

CADDY: You two are not showing much compassion right now.
 *(Pause)*
You have no idea what traumas he's suffered, what emotional pain he has endured.
 *(Pause)*
You both have your second chance. He deserves one, too.

*(RUDY sits up.)*

RUDY:
 *(Sings)*
I once was lost but now I'm found, / was blind, but now I see.

(*MIMI lights up and joins in, belting out the song.*)

RUDY AND MIMI:
    (*Sing*)
Amazing Grace! How sweet the sound / That saved a wretch like me! I once was lost but now am found, / was blind, but now I see.

(*Red lights flash through the room.*)

45:
    (*to Rudy*)
Your ride's here, friend.
    (*Pause*)
Our revels now are ended.

(*45 stands and helps RUDY to his feet. RUDY puts his hand on 45's shoulder. The doorbell chimes. The lights come down.*)

www.ingramcontent.com/pod-product-compliance
Lightning Source LLC
Chambersburg PA
CBHW020948090426
42736CB00010B/1323